Developing Personal Integrity

2nd Edition

Samuel Blankson

DEVELOPING PERSONAL INTEGRITY

This book is a work of non-fiction. Names of people and places have been changed to protect their privacy.

Copyright © 2005, by Samuel Blankson. All rights reserved including the right to reproduce this book, or portions thereof, in any form except for the inclusion of brief quotations in a review.

ISBN 1-4116-2376-2

Dedications

To God, my wife Uju, and all the leaders from IBS who taught me the meaning of integrity.

DEVELOPING PERSONAL INTEGRITY

Contents

Dedications v
Contents vii
Introduction 1
   Why I Am Writing This Book 3
Chapter 1 7
   Defining Integrity 7
      Understanding Integrity 9
      Definition of Integrity 13
      Integrity: the Components of the Definition 15
         Steadfast Adherence 15
         Being Unimpaired and Undivided 16
         Continuously Improving 17
Chapter 2 19
   The Founding Principles of Integrity 19
      Establishing Principles 21
         Love 22
         Honesty 22
         Faith and Hope 23
         Prudence 25
         Justice 25
         Fortitude 26
         Charity 26
         Temperance 27
Chapter 3 31
   Adhering Steadfastly to Your Principles 31
      Integrating the Principles into Your Life 33
         Love 34
         Honesty 34
         Faith and Hope 34
         Prudence 34
         Justice 35
         Fortitude 35
         Charity 35
         Temperance 36
      Avoiding Obstacles of Integrity 37
         Helplessness 38

Your Past	38
Old Beliefs	38
Your Emotional State	39
Sloth	41
Pride	41
Envy	42
Wrath	42
Desire	42
Covetousness and Lust	45
Gluttony	45
Your Environment	48
Home	48
Work	49
Family and Friends	49
Clubs and Associations	50
The Media	50
Improving Your Adherence to Your Principles	52
Hope and Enthusiasm	52
Attitude	53
Mentors	54
Books and Literature, Tapes, and Seminars	54
Associations	55

Chapter 4 59

Making Principles Unimpaired and Undivided 59

Guarding Against Integrity Erosion	61
Contradictions	61
Criticising, Comparing and Complaining	63
Criticising	63
Comparing	64
Complaining	65
Making Allowances for Your Benefit	68
Your Thoughts	69
Your Mind	69
Visualisation	70
Self-Talk	71

Chapter 5 75

Dedication to Continuous Improvement 75

Monitoring Your Adherence to Your Principles	77
Regularly Reviewing Your Progress	79
Consistently Working on Raising Your Level of Adherence to Your Principles	79

CONTENTS

Summary *83*
Appendix A *86*
Bibliography *87*
Notes *91*
Other Works By Samuel Blankson *93*
About The Author *112*

"... as with all great endeavours, the harder the struggle the greater the victory and personal growth"

Introduction

In the field of human character development, integrity is the last frontier. Many people use the word, but few really know what real integrity is. This book breaks down the fundamental components of personal integrity, and offers a path to attaining it.

Like success or happiness, integrity is a journey not a destination. We can only judge the measure of how far on the path we are through the observation of our inner voice, the voice of our conscience, and through deep contemplation and reflection.

Like a pearl, integrity has many layers, and the removal of a blemished layer reveals a newer layer to be removed. However, unlike the pearl, which diminishes in size and value when layers are removed, we grow in integrity through the removal of elements that compromise our integrity.

This journey of personal excellence is not an easy one. As a friend once said, "When peeling this onion, sometimes you cry." But in all great endeavours, the harder the struggle, the greater the victory and personal growth.

> *"The wider you read, the more you see the importance of integrity in attaining real happiness and success"*

INTRODUCTION

Why I Am Writing This Book

My interest and struggles in personal growth begun at age 7, while playing truant from school. I entered a public library on my way to school, and discovered Enid Blyton's wonderful children's fictional books.

The lifestyle and adventures of the children in her books fascinated me, and I read almost all her books by the time I was 14.

Blessed with this love for reading, I set out to devour any other books I could get my hands on.

By the time I was 19, I had discovered self-help and personal development books. I devoured these in search of clues to personal happiness, success, and excellence.

The more I read, the more I saw the importance of integrity in attaining real happiness and success.

As I worked on developing integrity in the various areas of my life (as a student, a boyfriend, a son, a brother, a friend, as an employer, and more), I became happier within myself, and developed character and self-assuredness.

I also gained the respect of others. People started to seek my advice on sensitive personal issues and I grew in leadership. I found people twice my age and more, choosing to follow me in various business enterprises.

As my responsibilities grew, I needed to operate with even higher levels of integrity. Levels of integrity that I had not understood previously, became a way of life. My new goals in integrity became increasingly challenging, but I had grown into a leader who could handle them.

The level of joy in my life soared. I started to love what I did. My businesses benefited with growth, and my relationship with my wife improved diametrically.

I grow in integrity every day, and sometimes, past issues tackled without integrity come back to educate me.

These experiences humble me and educate me. I have grown to look forward to these lessons, and to implementing them in my life. I then attain a higher level of self-respect, sense of achievement, and happiness through that growth.

I know where I have come from and where I am going. I also know that I am not much different from you. All I have done, you too can do, and more. Integrity is the key to real happiness and success. You may have success without integrity, but you will not have happiness.

Therefore, I hope and pray that you read this book, and apply the knowledge within it to your life. You will see the difference immediately in the way you feel about yourself, and later in how people feel about you. With time, all aspects of your life will also benefit.

INTRODUCTION

"Sometimes, past issues tackled without integrity come back to educate you"

Chapter 1

Defining Integrity

"To expect to achieve success in anything without commitment, responsibility, action, and inconvenience, is like attempting to drive your car without fuel"

Understanding Integrity

Today many people like to avoid commitments and responsibilities. We like to leave a back door open in all our pursuits to allow for a change of mind. Words like "commitment" can scare us from doing the right thing for our future, and we would rather settle for an easier life without commitments, responsibilities, and inconveniences.

This route leads to mediocrity and failure in life. Let me explain more.

All great achievers in history including great achievers in your life (perhaps your parents, an uncle, or an aunt) made commitments, took responsibility, took action, and suffered inconveniences to earn the respect and admiration that you have for them today.

To be successful in establishing integrity in your life, you will require commitment, responsibility, action, and you will experience inconvenience. To expect to achieve success in anything without commitment, responsibility, action, and inconvenience, is like attempting to drive your car without fuel. You will get nowhere fast (unless you start on a steep hill). Even if you started on a step hill your success will be short lived, and the person with fuel in their car will overtake you, and achieve more.

Taking responsibility and committing with action will introduce inconveniences and challenges in your life, but something else more important will also happen to you. You will come alive and grow to overcome these challenges. Whilst you are taking action, the inconveniences will diminish in importance.

When you are standing still in the rain, there are many inconveniences. You will get cold and wet. However, if you are running in the same downpour with a destination in mind, you will not notice how wet you are getting, as you will be busy running, and the rain will not have the same effect on you.

In both examples, the inconveniences are the same. However, as you can see, taking action, responsibility, and committing to get somewhere diminishes the inconveniences along the way.

You can apply this directly with your life. The weeks or days leading to most people's vacation are filled with activity. You have paid for the tickets and committed to go. You are responsible for packing your luggage, and for being ready at the airport on time. You do not even notice the inconveniences that you normally would during this time. All you can see is the goal of lying on that beach in total relaxation.

Integrity requires you to commit to adhere steadfastly to a set of strict moral or ethical codes. With this commitment will come challenges, expect them. In fact, as soon as you commit to something, you open the floodgate for challenges to test your resolve.

Expect them. Do not be surprised if you decide to stop swearing for instance, that you are cut up in traffic more so than usual, and have the urge to return to your old ways of responding.

You also have to become unimpaired and undivided in carrying out your commitment. It is not integrity if you only adhere to your moral or ethical codes under special conditions. Imagine telling or being told by your wife that she would be faithful to you 364 days of each year. Is that faithfulness?

Cohesion in your adherence to your moral or ethical code is very important, but not easy. When you start, you may slip up frequently. Nevertheless, recommit and start again, learning from your past setback, and with time you will experience less frequent backslides. I have found this to be true for myself. I used to be undisciplined with time keeping, often turning up an hour late for appointments, or not at all. When I decided to become punctual, I had many challenges. My car broke down, accidents on the roads seemed to increase, and my clocks and watch batteries seemed to all run out around this same time.

I was so tempted to give up on improving this character flaw, as the difficulties were great. Nevertheless, I persisted, and now I have good punctuality. In addition to this, if unavoidably delayed, I now always call ahead to notify and reschedule. I am still not perfect, but I am happier and less stressed and guilt ridden about my punctuality. In fact, it is now one of my positive personality traits that I am proud of and people frequently comment on.

Nevertheless, even in this I had to work on being unimpaired and undivided. You see, when I became punctual, I still maintained a lack of punctuality with my sisters. I suppose I took them for granted, and they never complained as they expected that behaviour from me. It was my wife who spotted this flaw in my character and helped me eliminate it. I could not operate with integrity when I was punctual with everyone except for my sisters. Cohesion in integrity is everything.

Integrity degrades with time if you do not maintain a vigilant improvement program. In life, there is no standing still. You are either moving ahead or sliding back. Resting on Laurel may have been Hardy's way of getting sleep, but it will destroy all the work you have done on your integrity if you rest on your laurels.

This brings me to my last point in what integrity is. The Japanese have a word "Kaizen," which means continuous improvement. This perfectly describes this final component of integrity. We continuously have to seek to improve our integrity. For example, if you have already decided not to lie, and have reached a point where you do not lie to mislead people, you could improve yourself even further. You could include white lies and any unlawful actions, like speeding when no speeding cameras or police are about.

Definition of Integrity

Now we come to my definition of integrity. This definition comprises of all the points discussed above. In the following chapters, we will dissect this definition, and find how we can implement integrity in everyday life.

Definition of Integrity: "The <u>steadfast adherence</u> to a strict moral or ethical code, the state of <u>being unimpaired and undivided</u> in this, and <u>continuously improving</u> on this state."

"Integrity is the steadfast adherence to a strict moral or ethical code, the state of being unimpaired and undivided in its continuous application, whilst constantly improving on this state"

Integrity: the Components of the Definition

From the definition on integrity, you can see the process by which integrity is acquired:

1. Through <u>steadfast adherence</u> to a strict moral or ethical code.
2. Through <u>being unimpaired and undivided</u> in this <u>steadfast adherence</u> to a strict moral or ethical code.
3. Through <u>continuously improving</u> on <u>being unimpaired and undivided</u> in the <u>steadfast adherence</u> to a strict moral or ethical code.

So let us take each element separately.

Steadfast Adherence
This means committing to adhere to moral or ethical codes steadfastly, being persistent, consistent, and operating with unwavering conviction. It means taking action to adhere to them determinedly.

These points are covered in more detail in Chapters 2 and 3, where you will do the following:

- Learn how to define your principles through a set of moral and ethical codes.
- Learn how to commit to your principles.

- Learn techniques and solutions to dealing with the challenges and setbacks that you will face after committing to your principles.
- Learn various actions that you can take right now to determinedly adhere to your principles.

Being Unimpaired and Undivided

You become impaired and divided when you do not believe that you can succeed in achieving a goal, and if you do not see or have any motivation or reward for achieving the goal. This may not be the direct cause for lack of integrity, however, without being unimpaired and undivided in your morals and ethics, doubt can set in. This can cause weakness in your character. You then start to develop excuses and justifications to slip away from your initial moral and ethical beliefs.

See Chapter 4 for techniques on how to protect your principles from the following:

- Impairment and division.
- Self-image erosion.
- Contradictions in your character.
- Negative actions and thoughts.
- Fears.
- Bad habits
- Bad associations

and more...

Continuously Improving

The vigilant student will constantly look for ways to improve whatever they are doing. In the arena of character building and integrity development, constant improvement is of the highest importance.

Chapter 5 covers how to maintain and continuously improve your level of integrity through the following:

- Monitoring your current level of integrity.
- Reviewing your development progress.
- Consistently raising your level of integrity.
- Rewarding yourself for all significant new levels of integrity reached.

"In the arena of character building and integrity development, constant improvement is of the highest importance"

Chapter 2

The Founding Principles of Integrity

"Within each of us lies a seed of truth, which seeks and recognises only its own kind"

Establishing Principles

We all have different views on what is important in our lives. Some people do not think that it is essential to be honest in business; however, dishonesty in personal relationships is unforgivable to them. What I aim to achieve in this book, is a set of principles that are universal and cohesive. These principles support and complement each other. Without them, there would be division, and the whole concept of integrity would crumple and fail under scrutiny.

Within each of us lies a seed of truth, which seeks and recognises only its own kind. The voice tells us when something is right or wrong. We call this the conscience. Sometimes we ignore this inner voice for so long that we do not hear it anymore, unless it screams.

However, we can start listening to this voice again, and increase its volume and feed its source by operating and leading our lives with integrity. When we lead our lives with integrity, our conscience grows stronger, and we can discern the finer signals that may have been lost previously by ignoring the small voice of truth within.

The following are the key principles required in establishing integrity:

- Love
- Honesty
- Faith and Hope
- Prudence

- Justice
- Fortitude
- Charity
- Temperance

Let us look at each of principles in detail.

Love

So what are these universal principles, you may ask. I believe they are all founded on Love. Almost all religions today advocate loving yourself and your neighbours. If you truly love someone, you will naturally operate with integrity with him or her. Learning to love all of our acquaintances will make living with integrity easier. I believe that out of love, flows all virtues.

Honesty

Honesty, being sincere, open, and truthful, is another corner stone of integrity. Honesty is a fundamental that we cannot ignore if we want a life of happiness. I remember an old friend telling me once, the best way to not be caught in a lie is to tell the truth. Honesty, like its opposite dishonesty, grows easier to apply when frequently used. You never need to remember what you said if you tell the truth. When questioned on it years later, you will only need to recall the truth, instead of trying to recall the web of lies upon lies that you have woven, in order to avoid exposing yourself as a liar.

Honest people do not live a lie, so they have no need to prove their honesty constantly. Liars on the other hand, have to prove their honesty constantly, and waste vital resources in planning and remembering what to say, and what they have said previously.

Today, the lives of most role models and worldwide leaders do not represent a life of honesty. Politicians often weave words to please voters, rather than tell the truth and risk loosing elections. They are eventually found out as liars and instead of telling the truth, they attempt to place blame elsewhere and forfeit responsibility for their actions.

Faith and Hope

Faith and hope is vital when you or others are going through challenges. You need to lead a life that inspires trust and loyalty, and therefore live your life with conviction. People will not trust you or have faith in you if you speak or act without conviction. You need to operate with fidelity in order to inspire belief in others and in yourself. To be relied on by others, you will need to offer hope through how you live your life.

> *"...treat all living things with fairness and impartiality"*

Prudence

Today, prudence is disregarded by our consumer-orientated society. We are encouraged to spend without thought and keep up with the rapidly changing product lines being pushed at us constantly. However, it is not just with money that we need to exercise this wisdom. Many of us engage in dangerous life threatening habits such as smoking, excessive drinking, drug abuse, casual sex, and pornography. Many of us talk, act, and wear clothing that is not discrete. We may drive without care for our lives and other road users. Lack of prudence will erode your integrity and corrupt your character from the inside out.

Justice

To treat all living things with fairness and impartiality comes back to the foundation of love. All prejudices and racial hatred stem from a great lack in this fundamental, Justice. Do the right thing because it is right. Be non-judgemental and fair to all living things. Apply equity to all your thoughts and relationships with others. Trying to understand other people's points of view is not an easy exercise. However, we can learn this habit with practice.

I recall a friend who was going through difficulties with his marriage. He started seeing another woman outside of his relationship. I judged him and categorised him as such, without seeking to understand his challenges. Years later, I discovered some facts that changed my view of him. Had I been open-minded and fair in dealing with him, I could have helped him better. Instead, my harsh treatment pushed him further into the dark.

Fortitude

You will need courage and endurance to stick to your resolutions. A weak will is tormented by every shadow, and disturbed by every noise. However, a strong courageous spirit operating with fortitude will see you through when challenges and difficulties beset you. The prize in this case, goes those with strength of character and endurance. You may fail many times before you overcome some weaknesses, but never give up.

Charity

The benevolence, mercy, and helpfulness of a charitable heart, is another part of the foundation of integrity that many discard. If you are being fair, how can you turn your eyes away from the suffering? How can you be doing well, but see a suffering soul and not show mercy? Integrity requires us to show mercy and kindness to all. This is not only with our money. Charity can be shown and practised in many ways.

We can give our ideas, our energy, our time, our money, our home, and our prayer. Sometimes, a word of praise or a smile is appreciated more than a wallet full of cash. Make it a habit to greet people with a smile. Be generous with your words of praise, and seek to understand people when they are talking. Congratulate the deserved and uplift the downhearted. Many acts of charity are free, but can make such a difference to others, and in what you get in return from others. However, be warned, be sincere. Do not smile or use charity in order to manipulate others.

Temperance

With everything, exercise in moderation. One of the things my brother was fond of saying when we were growing up was, "Too much of anything is bad for you." There is so much truth in this. Today, we do so much to excess. Our society has become more focused on pleasure and leisure. We are constantly seeking sources of pleasure, and avoiding sobriety and the moderate lifestyle. We want to drink to excess, have faster cars, have bigger homes, and take more vacations. We want to be right all the time, and many of us are overweight from lack of self-control in our diets.

We need to change our lifestyles to represent a life of self-mastery. You can take control of your life with this magic word, "NO." Say no to excess. When the sales person tries to convince you to buy something out of your financial range, and in excess of your needs, say "NO." When your drinking friends ask you to come down the pub or bar for the fourth night in a week say "NO." Say "NO" to excess amounts of fatty junk foods. This is not easy to do. However, by making the change, you will be rewarded with a healthier body and a stronger will. These long lasting rewards by far outweigh the price you will have to pay by not making the change.

Temperance has the following components:

- Physical – excessive drinking, smoking, excessive eating, unhealthy sexual habits, etc.
- Attitude – always wanting more but never appreciating what you have.
- Talking – Speaking more than you listen.
- Waste – excessive spending and throwing away good things just because you want to have the latest.
- Emotional - harbouring hatred and anger. Flaring up, doing and saying things you do not mean.

The lesson with temperance is simple: you cannot find happiness outside your own mind. If you are trying to find a spouse, a new home, a new job, move to a different country etc, in order to be happy, I have bad news for you. You will get a spouse, a new home, a new job and move country, but you will keep your unhappiness.

An unhappy environment may not be responsible for you not smiling, or you being are a negative wreck. You could probably find a happy person in that same environment. Seek happiness in your mind first, and then change your external circumstances to match. You will be surprised to find that by changing your internal state of mind, you will automatically change your external state.

THE FOUNDING PRINCIPLES OF INTEGRITY

"Seek happiness in your mind first, and then change your external circumstances"

Chapter 3

Adhering Steadfastly to Your Principles

"Avoid extremes in all your undertakings"

Integrating the Principles into Your Life

You now have the principles with which to live your life. Your foundation for integrity has been established. You can start now, and with that beginning, plant the seed to grow an orchard of integrity.

Go through each one of the fundamentals below and ask yourself, "Can I commit to integrate and steadfastly apply these principles in my life?" You may not be able to reach the pinnacle for each of these fundamentals, but you can at least decide to improve on them over time.

Love
- Love yourself.
- Love all other people.
- Love all other creatures.
- Love the environment.

Honesty
- Speak only what you know is the truth.
- Act with honestly. Do not engage in anything that you suspect or know is dishonest, unlawful, or immoral. This includes not harming or misleading others or yourself.
- Do not hide behind silence. If you know the truth, and know it will help someone in trouble, communicate it.

Faith and Hope
- Uphold your spiritual beliefs unless they speak against loving others.
- Believe in yourself and others. Have faith in yourself. Empower others with belief in themselves.
- Listen to others to understand their desires and encourage them to achieve them.
- Have a dream or goal that you are working on, which will help others and yourself.

Prudence
- Think before you speak or act. Avoid being rash in your words. Think through all your decisions, and sleep on them if possible.

- Avoid environments or people who seek to harm you.
- Avoid debt. When possible, save, and pay with cash. If you are always in debt, seek to pay your debtors as soon as possible.

Justice
- Treat everyone with fairness.
- Do not judge. If you have to, judge with impartiality.
- Do not assume; always ask for clarification.
- Always do the right thing legally and morally, for the good of yourself and all involved.

Fortitude
- If the idea is sound, never give up on it.
- Fear only what can kill you. Eliminate irrational fears from your character.
- Always give it all you have. Go the extra mile.
- Be strong-minded. Avoid people who pull you down. Associate with people who uplift you, and who are strong-willed and determined.

Charity
- Give at least 10% of your take home income to a cause that you believe in, that does not harm you, others, or the environment.
- Greet everyone with a smile.
- Show interest in others and seek to understand them.

- Give your time to a cause that you believe in that helps others.
- Be first to complement and praise others.

Temperance
- Do not do anything to the point that it controls you negatively.
- Avoid extremes: drugs, drink, sex, etc.
- Listen more than you talk.

Avoiding Obstacles of Integrity

With time and lack of maintenance, attrition will set in. This is true for integrity. You cannot acquire a high level of integrity and just leave it. It will slowly erode and you will backslide into lower levels of integrity. You can loose integrity faster than you will ever acquire it. It makes sense to support, maintain, and feed it regularly.

You will need to guard yourself from some enemies. These enemies are ruthless and cunning. They will never tire, and will keep persisting until you give in. You cannot destroy them, but you can suppress their influence to levels where they have no power over you.

Watch out for these following enemies:

- Helplessness
- Your Past
- Old beliefs
- Your emotional state
- Sloth
- Pride
- Envy
- Wrath
- Desire
- Your environment

Now let us take a closer look at each of these enemies.

Helplessness

The first enemy, helplessness, has a special power source. It gets its power from the belief that you are controlled by your environment and other external sources. To destroy helplessness, you need to develop a sense of control over your life. If you believe that you are happy, sad, rich, poor, or unlucky because of external events or other people's beliefs, then you are an easy target for helplessness.

Take control of your life, assume responsibility for how you feel and the actions you take. When you understand that you are responsible for how you feel, that you control how you feel, and that you control whether you succeed or fail in your life, you become free of helplessness. You gain a freedom only enjoyed by the mentally liberated. You can change something in your life to affect every situation. If it is raining, you can decide to be happy regardless of the rain. Take an umbrella or enjoy the free shower.

Your Past

The beliefs you associate with your past experiences can control you in your present. You may have learned helplessness in your past if you found yourself in a helpless position, and believed that you would always be helpless in similar situations forever.

Old Beliefs

You may harbour old beliefs that hold you back. For example, you may have been told as a child that you were lazy, stupid, or clumsy. Now, in your adulthood, you are still demonstrating this behaviour because you think and believe that you cannot change it. I have good news for you. This is not the truth.

You can change your beliefs. Take action, and with time, your self-image will catch up.

Decide to take action now. With repeated action, the fear will disappear.

Your Emotional State

Your environment does not create your emotional states, you do. You cannot control the trains being late, the weather being foul, or your spouse waking up in the morning with a bad mood. If you use these outside occurrences as a thermostat to set your temperature, then you forfeit control of your life to them. Your interpretation of external occurrences produces your belief system. Take control of your life, assume responsibility for how you feel and the actions you take.

"…helplessness has a special power source. It gets its power from the belief that you are controlled by your environment and other external sources"

Sloth

Laziness can often cause you to act without integrity. If you find yourself lying, procrastinating, and shirking your duties, it could be because you are not industrious. If you are holding back from carrying out your duties, then you are acting without integrity.

Over time, this habit will lead to loss of trust and respect from others. You will not be asked to perform any important duties because you will have shown in the past that either you lacked the integrity to carry out that responsibility, or you delivered poor quality results through your work or from your actions. Seek to curtail this habit early by acting promptly on your responsibilities and duties, and going the extra mile in all your undertakings. The person who will loose out when you shirk your responsibilities will be you.

Pride

If you are arrogant, conceited, and full of self-importance, this will hinder your growth. I have found that people like this are often hiding a deep-seated low self-image. They want to be respected because they do not respect themselves. They act as if they are better than others are because they think they themselves are not important. Developing a strong self-image and humility, you will loose these bad traits.

Envy

Feeling envious and jealous of others is a sure sign that you do not believe in yourself, or that you can achieve the same. For example, you may be envious of someone that earns more money than you do. All these reasons have one root, lack of self-belief and self-respect. People who love themselves and are happy within themselves cannot be envious of others or their possessions. Work on yourself, and your problems involving others will disappear.

Wrath

You may be aggressive because in your past, you may have learned to be this way in order to survive. Through your past victimisation, you may have learned to defend yourself with aggressive behaviour. This obstacle of integrity will undermine your good work in developing integrity. This is because the respect that you build up in yourself and others can be destroyed by a temper tantrum, or angry words spoken without thought. Guard against your temper. Remember the first fundamental, Love.

Desire

Our desires if unchecked can grow to consume us. If you are of a covetous nature, you may undermine your personal integrity through greed, adultery, or some other way. Not being satisfied with what you have and wanting what belongs to someone else, is a bad habit. It can destroy your name or even ruin your life if unchecked. Do not try to compete with the Joneses. The best way to get over this habit is to learn to appreciate what you have, and work on improving your situation for yourself, rather than comparing yourself to others.

"With repeated action, the fear will disappear"

Covetousness and Lust

One aspect of covetousness and lust is sexual promiscuity. This is perhaps the most dangerous enemy today, as it could lead to the acquisition of sexually transmitted diseases, and that could end your life prematurely. Breaking trust in relationships through sexual promiscuity causes unnecessary hurt and pain. If you have a problem with your sexual desires, seek professional help before it consumes you and causes you to loose integrity.

Gluttony

Greed is very common today. Various lotteries and casinos make their living from this weakness in human nature. The press and media seem to encourage greed by highlighting how much people can have, which emphasizes how little you have. This can cause you to want more just for the sake of keeping up appearances.

Contrary to popular belief, the vast majority of wealthy people are not greedy. To get to where they are, they had to apply sound financial judgement and patience. They had a dream and chased it to fruition. The act of chasing a dream humbles you, and lets you see how deserved the successful are.

If you are greedy, I advise you get a dream. If you expect something for nothing, you will always want more than you deserve. Find something that you believe in, and put all your energies into it. You will not be greedy for long because you will not succeed if you are. Use hard honest work for all your desire, and greed will never knock at your door.

"Work on yourself, and your problems involving others will disappear"

Your Environment

It is important for you to control all variables that affect your integrity. The environment you live in often shapes you in subtle ways. Is your home a place where you can grow in integrity, or are you living in an environment that violates any of the fundamentals of integrity? Often, you may have problems at home that you have allowed to get so bad that the home becomes a place of hatred and resentment. This is not a place for integrity to grow. You must change this if that is how you are living now.

Home

Resentment can be resolved or healed through love. By listening and seeking to understand your partner, children, or whoever you live with without judging them, you can bring about peace and joy to your home.

If you are the adult in your household, remember that you set the example of integrity for everyone. This is a great responsibility, and you should feel honoured by it. You set the example for your children, and you will influence them more than anyone else will. Therefore, set an example that will make you proud of yourself.

This also means being extra careful with how you react, and with the things you do. You send conflicting messages to the family when you drive through red lights and speed over the legal speed limits after telling your children not to commit crime. "Daddy is a liar," or "Daddy doesn't have integrity," will be on their minds, although you may never hear them say this.

Work

Sometimes, the work environment is a breeding ground for integrity erosion. Do not associate with the gossipers. Have the guts to stand up to what you believe in. If someone is spreading rumours to you about someone else, speak up and say, "Why don't you tell them to their face? You will get a better result than talking to me about it."

Family and Friends

Integrity takes time to filter through, but with persistence and application, soon your friends and family will start acting with integrity around you. They will respect you too much to do otherwise. I found this to be true in my own case. People who know me do not swear or gossip around me. They know that I will not stand for that. You will earn their respect when they see that your integrity is not just for show.

Clubs and Associations

Sometimes you may belong to a club or association that encourages some of your bad habits. If this is the case, you will need to disassociate from them until you are strong enough in your level of integrity to be unaffected by them. In my personal experiences, I have never found a time when I was too strong to be affected by bad associations.

The Media

A great source of corruption for the average person today is the media. In order to sell more copies, media companies will often distort the truth or over sensationalise a minority view. Some specialise in blatant lies, gossip, bad news, or pornography. Perhaps the worst case here is pornographic media. Beware of integrity corrupters in the media.

Beware of taking in copious amounts of bad news. We live in a world where you can get information about any event around the world within seconds of it occurring through television, radio, and the internet. Many still depend on the newspapers and television stations to feed them only the "bad news," when the internet can now be used to find the precise information we are looking for.

Today, I rarely listen to radio news, television news, or buy newspapers. Instead, I use the Internet a lot. Why? Because I can control the news and information that I consume. I do not want to hear of murders, rapes, killings, and riots every day. This negative news is at an imbalance with good news and achievements that receive little coverage. Seek to control what you watch and read. Otherwise, someone else will control it for you. Avoid watching television news or reading newspapers for 30 days, and judge for yourself the difference it makes to your life.

Improving Your Adherence to Your Principles

To ease your adherence to application of integrity, you will need to bolster your lifestyle with some defences. These defences will help you develop resilience to the negative influences that will attack your integrity.

Hope and Enthusiasm

Everything is easier when we do it with enthusiasm. Enthusiasm releases incredible forces that will help you to do more in less time, whilst having fun doing it.

So how do you get enthusiasm to defend your integrity? You use a reward system. This system is used greatly in goal setting. It is a simple system of assigning a reward to the attainment of a particular level of achievement. For instance, if you were working on controlling your sexual desires, a good goal would be not to flirt outside of your relationship for one month. When this was achieved, you could reward yourself with a trip to the cinema to see a film with your partner.

There are a few things to note about the reward technique as listed below:

1. Do not cheat by rewarding yourself, even if you do not succeed.

2. Do not make it too difficult to earn the reward. Your goal should push you to achieve it, without being unachievable. This allows you to build confidence and belief that you can do it.
3. Do not make the reward too small or too big. If it is too small, then you will not be motivated to achieve it. Moreover, if it is too big (expensive), you will not be able to use the reward technique for too long before your bankruptcy is inevitable.
4. Keep the goal and reward a secret. Telling other people and then failing may make you never want to do it again.

The reward system is your fuel. It will give you hope and enthusiasm. This fuel will power your integrity's defence mechanism.

Attitude

Your attitude is the thermostat that dictates your level of productivity and enjoyment of life. A negative attitude will result in negative thoughts and lack of confidence and belief in yourself. Just thinking negatively undermines the fundamental principles. You cannot be charitable, loving, or fair when you have a bad attitude. Developing a good attitude is essential to operating with integrity.

You can get an instant good attitude by changing the following:

1. Change your posture. Hold your body as if you are happy, and have a good attitude. Stick out your chest proudly, talk faster, smile

enthusiastically, walk faster, and breathe deeply.
2. Think of a situation or joke that makes you laugh.
3. Imagine yourself in a "happy place." This could be for example on holiday, or winning an award etc.
4. Move vigorously in order to increase your energy level. (Be careful if you are asthmatic or have related health problems).
5. Go and do something positive and fun, like swimming, playing with your kids, walking, or driving.

Mentors

Athletes use a coach to help them reach levels of excellence in their sport. Today, there are coaches and mentors for business and personal excellence. They can be costly, but they are worth their weight in gold. They encourage and help their clients focus their energies for greater productivity.

You can apply this principle of mentoring in your own life to increase our level of integrity. If there is someone in your life that embodies the principles that you wish to adopt, make their acquaintance and associate with them. By associating with them, their way of life will rub off on you. Be careful to choose worthy, well-rounded mentors who lead a balanced life.

Books and Literature, Tapes, and Seminars

Another type of association can be found in the form of the books you read, the audio media you listen to (CDs, DVDs, mini disks, tapes and videos), and the seminars and functions you attend. The power of this trio in influencing lives is immeasurable.

As I said at the beginning of this book, books changed my life from the early days. Today I read for at least an hour a day. I listen to audio media while I sleep, and for many hours whilst I am awake. I like to read motivational and self-help books. I keep them all around the house and in my brief case, so that while waiting for a bus, train, or during lunch, I can read something inspiring. I read in the lavatory, and I read instead of watching television. Reading 7 hours a week relates to 364 hours of positive input a year.

Audio media is a great skill teacher, and can be listened to in the car, or whilst working around the home. Today, there are countless thousands of audio media. These teach languages, people skills, motivation, abridged versions of classic books, and much more.

Most of the good authors also hold seminars, which you probably will find information on at the back of their books or on the internet. Through seminars, you can learn from experts in any field. The best in the world can teach you how to improve your marriage, your business, or countless hundreds of topics. I attend seminars and functions throughout the year on various topics.

Associations

The easiest way to go astray is to hang around with people who are acting without integrity, and learn

DEVELOPING PERSONAL INTEGRITY

to do as they do. No matter how hard you try, if you have bad associations and socialise with them, you will be doomed to failure in living with integrity.

I once worked with a man who was about to divorce his wife. I noticed that his brother and three of his best friends were all divorcees. This highlighted to me the power of association. Watch who you associate with, because in the next ten years, where you are will be due to the sum of what you have read, listened to, and the people you have associated with.

On the other hand, a strong social group of people leading lives of integrity, and actively seeking to improve themselves, will help you skyrocket your own growth. Therefore, choose your social group carefully.

ADHERING STEADFASTLY TO YOUR PRINCIPLES

"Watch who you associate with, for where you are in ten years will be due to the sum of what you have read, listened to, and the people you have associated with"

Chapter 4

Making Principles Unimpaired and Undivided

"...uncertainty arises when you operate without clear principles"

Guarding Against Integrity Erosion

Many things in the outside world can lead you from the path of integrity. You can avoid most of them by placing yourself in a different environment. However, some enemies gain their energies from within your mind, whilst others dwell there.

They attach themselves to your mind, making you vacillate, and cause your principles to disintegrate. They introduce the number one enemy of success, doubt. We will now examine some of these subtle negative traits in detail, and discuss ways to destroy them.

Contradictions

Have you ever wanted to do something but were not sure if it was right or wrong? This uncertainty arises when you operate without clear principles. When you raise a minor and non-fundamental belief to match the importance of one of your fundamentals, you will experience contradictions in your character.

For instance, if you believe that you must always be right, this belief will contradict a fundamental. A practical example of this contradiction would be if you tell your daughter not to lie, when you do. When she questions you about the time she heard you lying to your boss on the telephone about being sick in order to take the day off work, you dismiss your own lies.

The bad thing about contradictions although you may not realise it, is that as they increase in occurrence, your integrity diminishes accordingly. You may feel as though you have a high level of integrity, but everyone else may think differently. To find out how you rank to other people as a person with integrity, humble yourself and ask them.

Once you recognise the contradicting belief that is usurping your integrity, take action immediately to reverse the damage. Apologise to the relevant people for being a hypocrite, and commit to change. Whenever you find yourself doing it again, reverse the action or words immediately.

For instance, if you tell people that you are fair and just, and you catch yourself acting unfairly or unjustly, correct it immediately and do the right thing. Similarly, aim to never criticize, and if you catch yourself in a moment of anger criticizing your spouse, apologise to him or her immediately, and guard against it in the future.

The steps for handling contradictions in your integrity are a follows:
1. Identify the contradiction.
2. Apologise to relevant person.
3. Commit to eradicate the cause of the contradiction.
4. Look out vigilantly for these occurrences in the future. Ask family and friends to help you by pointing out whenever you stray. This will help keep you on track.

Contradictions in character and integrity are subtle. Sometimes you will not notice them. It is always a good idea to ask someone you trust like your spouse or a friend to help you identify these contradictions in your character.

It is important to apologise when you are wrong or when you have unknowingly offended someone. By you apologising and committing to make a change for the better, others will change the image they have of you. This will make it easier for you to stick to your new commitment to change, because other people's negative beliefs about you will often cause you to act accordingly, thus hindering your efforts.

Criticising, Comparing and Complaining

"The three C's" will undermine your integrity and cause you to become a hypocrite in other people's eyes.

Criticising

The act of non-constructive criticism requires the person being criticised to be torn down. Unless this is followed by words of unconditional love and encouragement, the criticism can be destructive.

To destroy another person or your own self-image is not fair, charitable, honest, or an act of love. It goes against the fundamentals of integrity. It is easy to criticise others when we feel they have done wrong, especially against us. This form of criticism is often based on a defensive and spiteful reaction to a perceived personal attack. You should guard against this. If you cannot say anything positive or encouraging, you should say nothing.

More often than not, people realise when they are wrong, and will seek advice from you if they feel they can talk to you without being judged and criticised. Like a clam, criticism causes people to close their minds and hearts.

We are all unique human beings, different in so many ways. You cannot be compared with anyone else, because you are different in so many ways. Even the cells in our bodies are individual and different in so many ways.

Comparing

It is never right to compare people. You may compare their actions to help them get better results, but do not compare them as human beings. There are some inherent factors in all human beings that cannot be changed. Two examples of these factors are your parentage and race. Comparing people on things that they cannot change can only be destructive and damaging to them, and to your integrity.

We often compare people in order to highlight weaknesses in them or in ourselves. The mistake of comparing other people's strengths against your weaknesses or visa versa, can only lead to feelings of inadequacy, or pride, the opposite of humility. This act does not support integrity.

Instead of comparing yourself with others, try comparing yourself today with yourself yesterday. The differences may encourage you, or highlight where you need to make changes. Comparing yourself now with where you want to be in the future can help you stay on course and keep focused.

Complaining

When faced with a problem, you have choices. You can seek a solution, complain, or do nothing. The former is the desired action. Doing nothing increases the impact or effects of the problem. Complaining amplifies the problem, and you become part of the problem.

Complainers drive people away from themselves and make enemies of potential friends and allies. It is said that no one likes a complainer, not even other complainers. This is because complainers sap life out of situations. They drain the colour from life.

Constant complaining as a habit is very destructive to your self-image and success in anything you undertake. You will not get the help you seek, nor see the potential opportunities when you focus on complaining all the time about the negatives.

Seasoned complainers do not need negative situations to complain, as they can complain about positive conditions too. For example, have you ever heard anyone complaining about the weather when it is sunny and warm? Or, have you head anyone complaining about how much tax they would have to pay if they got a pay rise?

You cannot be positive and a complainer at the same time. Complaints cause inconsistencies in your character in striving towards integrity, making your acts and words lack cohesion. Avoid complainers, and guard against doing this yourself.

"Complaints cause inconsistencies in your character in striving towards integrity, making your acts and words lack cohesion"

Making Allowances for Your Benefit

Sometimes we can fall in love with the benefits of being seen to have integrity. If you seek to become a person viewed by others as having integrity, rather than a person who knows within themselves that you have integrity, you will open yourself to corruption from within. It will not be long before others expose you for who you really are.

To guard against this you must understand the title of this book "*Developing Personal Integrity.*" You are developing PERSONAL integrity, not a social or societal one. We do not want to appear as a person with high integrity if we are not, because that deception in itself makes you not a person of integrity, but a charlatan.

To be happy with yourself you must be honest with yourself. Honesty is universal and cannot be removed from certain situations or in dealing with certain people as you please. You are either honest or you are not.

If you seek to impress or manipulate other people through a façade of insincere integrity, you will only loose self-respect. Eventually, you will loose the respect and trust of all the people you misled.

You must not use integrity as a tool to acquire nepotism, material possessions, or position. These things are earned through honest and sincere application of the fundamentals for integrity.

In seeing the benefits of a life led with integrity, some will start to abuse the trust they have earned. If you see these signs within yourself, root them out immediately, or they will grow to consume you.

Your Thoughts

Social image has been raised to high levels of individual priority today, including in children. The purchase of a certain car or pair trainers, allows for an appropriate shift in one's image. This vacillation in your image can cause you to act without integrity.

A bad attitude is also fashionable today. Travelling on the underground or subway systems highlight the adoption of most passengers wearing a 'sour' face, and pushing and shoving without apology. You may normally be a cheerful, quick to smile, and courteous person, but by adopting the subway attitude, you behave and react just like others around you. This may lead you to act out of integrity.

Watch out for people, situations, and things that cause you to change your attitude or personality to "fit in," or "to be seen as belonging." Shallow fake characters break the fundamental of Honesty. Always be yourself. Being unsure of yourself will cause you to fall for anything.

If you do not decide who you are, someone else will give you an identity and set of beliefs and principles to live by. The media and your associates will all be glad to add their belief systems to yours, when you are unsure of what you stand for.

Your Mind

Your mind is comprised of a conscious element, and a more powerful subconscious element. The conscious element is the side of you that you are aware of all the time you are awake. It sleeps when you sleep.

The subconscious element handles your vital life systems like your breathing, heart regulation, cell growth, digestive system, and many such functions. It cannot differentiate reality from a vividly imagined picture.

That is why you can have all the reactions associated with a burglar breaking into your house when you hear a noise in the kitchen at night. Your mind will fill in the blanks, and in the case of the noise, you vividly imagine a burglar. Therefore, your mind and body react accordingly. If you believed it was your spouse making the noise, your mind and body would react differently.

That is part of the awesome power that your mind has. You can use the conscious to program the subconscious. We will now discuss two techniques that you can use to change your beliefs and habits, in order to facilitate achieving a higher level of integrity.

Visualisation

So how do you see yourself? Can you picture yourself acting and living with integrity? Use mental pictures to strengthen your self-image. Visualisation is the process by which astronauts, high achievers, athletes, and sportsmen use to see themselves winning before it actually happens. You can adopt this technique for strengthening your integrity and gaining success in the cleaning up of your bad habits.

Sit or lie somewhere quite and peaceful. Clear your mind of chatter, and picture yourself as you want to be. Imagine yourself in situations where you want to have more integrity. In the mental pictures, see yourself acting with total integrity. Feel how it will feel. Do this at least once when you awake, and again when you retire to bed. Very soon, you will be living the mental pictures that you visualised.

Self-Talk

The words we hear and speak make a difference. For instance, if you were repeatedly told that you were a failure, you would begin to fail at all things you undertook. That is why advertisers use repeated messages to sell their products. They know that even if you are not consciously paying attention, your subconscious mind will be hearing their messages. And sure enough, the next time you are in the supermarket you have an urge to try that new product.

We can use this same principle of repeated suggestions in integrity. Run an Ad Campaign on yourself. Tell yourself who you want to be in the present tense. For instance, you can say, "I am always punctual," or "I always tell the truth," or "I live my life with total integrity."

At first, your mind will fight the new image instruction, because it does not fit with the old one. But persistent repetition of the new instructions will yield results. You will soon see changes in how you react in situations where you lacked integrity previously.

Self-talk is most effective with regular repetition, preferably in front of a mirror. We believe ourselves more than we believe almost anyone else. Your mind will accept the new instructions as a fact when it hears it coming from you.

You can also record yourself saying these instructions, and play the recording in your car, around the house, or even as you sleep. Your subconscious mind, the part of the mind that never sleeps, will hear and change your self-image and beliefs accordingly.

I have used all of these techniques, and continue to use them. They always work, sometimes very quickly, other times over a period of months. The speed of results depends on the power of the belief you are trying to replace. A small and powerless belief can be replaced quickly, whilst beliefs that go back to our childhood require more time and repetition to replace.

MAKING PRINCIPLES UNIMPAIRED AND UNDIVIDED

"Use mental pictures to strengthen your self-image"

Chapter 5

Dedication to Continuous Improvement

"…actively raise your thinking and attitude through reading, listening, and observing role models"

Monitoring Your Adherence to Your Principles

Before you can accurately implement a positive change, it is best to acquire information on the current situation. This information can then be used to determine areas needing improvement. If integrity is to be maintained and improved upon, you need to know where you stand at present. You can acquire this information by monitoring yourself and noting down your progress.

I have provided a chart in Appendix A. Make copies of it, and use these charts weekly. Fill in your name and the date. When you begin, the week N° will be 1, and then every week after this, the number should increase by 2, 3, 4 and so on.

During the day as you go about your work and play, observe how you conduct yourself. In the violations column, note the amount of incidents where you violated your principles. Use any numbering style you prefer. You may wish to use a pencil so that you can make changes easily.

Working on all 8 principles will be difficult to undertake simultaneously, so choose one of the principles, and monitor yourself for 6 weeks. After 6 weeks, move on to the next principle and continue this until the final 6-week period. After 48 weeks, you will have monitored yourself on all the principles, and be in a position to review your statistics to determine where you need the most work, and where you need to focus on the least.

> *"You cannot allow yourself to think you have arrived, because after ripening comes decay"*

There is no right or wrong way to work on your principles. You can devise a system that better suits you, as long as you can work and improve on all of your principles with time.

Regularly Reviewing Your Progress

The process of acquiring the frequency of you violating these principles is to reduce the occurrence of these violations. Set violation goals for each principle, with the aim of reducing the violations gradually with every passing week. With every goal, attach a specific date and set a reward for its achievement.

Once a week, review your progress towards your goals. Visualise achieving your goals and earning the rewards.

Consistently Working on Raising Your Level of Adherence to Your Principles

The journey to integrity is fraught with obstacles. These must be overcome in order to make progress. Help is needed to develop the tenacity and courage to overcome these obstacles. This help comes in the form of your associations through books, tapes, functions, and mentors.

You have to actively raise your thinking and attitude through reading, listening, and observing your role models. You cannot allow yourself to think you have arrived, because after ripening comes decay. You have to stay 'green' and teachable. Be willing to learn from all sources.

I was talking to my niece about not swearing one day when she taught me a great lesson in humility. She told me that she sometimes swore at school and at home. I was shocked and immediately proceeded to explain to her the repercussions of swearing.

After talking for about ten minutes, I chanced to ask her what words she used when she swore. She told me "Gosh," and "Sugar." I realised that I should have been the one learning from this 13 year old. You see, I still used "real" swear words quite frequently at the time. I decided to change a few things in my life, especially listening more than talking.

Lessons and opportunities are everywhere if you are looking for them. You only need look, and you will find. Once uncovered, apply them immediately.

DEDICATION TO CONTINOUS IMPROVEMENT

"Lessons and opportunities are everywhere if you are looking for them. You only need look, and you will find. Once uncovered apply them immediately"

Summary

We began this book by defining integrity as "The steadfast adherence to a strict moral or ethical code, the state of being unimpaired and undivided in this, and continuously improving on this state." This definition was broken down in detail, in order to focus on each component in the definition.

Now you know what integrity is and how to acquire and maintain it, will you choose to develop it? I offer you a challenge. I challenge you to develop integrity in all the different areas of your life. I hope you take this challenge, as you will experience a more rewarding life by doing so.

By living your life with integrity, you will gain self-respect, and command respect in all your relationships. You will be sought out by those who seek trust and reliability, and your business and family life will both improve when you choose Developing Personal Integrity.

To end well, begin immediately

Appendix A
Principles Adherence Chart
Name:

Date:

Week Nº:

Principle	Aim	Violations	Note
Love	Love yourself, all other people, all other creatures and the environment.		
Honesty	Be sincere, open, lawful, and moral in your conduct.		
Faith & Hope	Believe in yourself and in others. Be optimistic and anticipate good.		
Prudence	Have discretion, good sense, and practice forethought in all you do.		
Justice	Be impartial, be fair, and unassuming.		
Fortitude	Have resilience, determination, strength of character, and courage in all you do.		
Charity	Give generously of yourself with love. Tithe at least 10% of your income.		
Temperance	Have balance in your life in all things, and avoid extremes in all that you do.		

Bibliography

The Holy Quran: An English Translation
by Allamah Nooruddin

Giant Steps
by Anthony Robbins

Unlimited Power
by Anthony Robbins

Grow Rich While You Sleep
by Ben Sweetland

The Teaching of Buddha
by Bukkyo Dendo Kyokai

Motivational Classics: Acres of Diamonds, the Kingship of Self Control, As a Man Thinketh
by Charles E. Jones

Magic of Believing
by Claude M. Bristol, Nido R. Qubein

TNT the Power Within You
by Claude M. Bristol, Harold Sherman

Don't Let Anybody Steal Your Dream
by Dexter Yager, Douglas Wood

Dynamic People Skills
by Dexter Yager, Ron Ball

Everything I Know at the Top I Learned at the Bottom
by Dexter Yager

Mark of Millionaire
by Dexter Yager

Millionaire Mentality
by Dexter Yager

Ordinary Men, Extraordinary Heroes
by Dexter Yager, Ron Ball

Wake Up and Live
by Dorothea Brande

Self Mastery Through Conscious Autosuggestion
by Emile Coue

The Richest Man in Babylon
by George S. Clason

Men Are From Mars, Women Are From Venus
by John Gray

Do It! A Guide to Living Your Dreams
by John-Roger and Peter McWilliams

BIBLIOGRAPHY

You can't afford the Luxury of a Negative Thought
by John-Roger and Peter McWilliams

How to Have Confidence and Power in Dealing With People
by Les Giblin

Napoleon Hill's Keys to Success: The 17 Principles of Personal Achievement
by Napoleon Hill, Matthew Sartwell

Think and Grow Rich
by Napoleon Hill

The Think and Grow Rich Action Pack
by Napoleon Hill

The Holy Bible Containing: King James Version
by National Publishing Company

Compassionate Capitalism: People Helping People Help Themselves
by Richard M. Devos,

Cashflow Quadrant: Rich Dad's Guide to Financial Freedom
by Robert T. Kiyosaki

Rich Dad's Guide to Investing: What the Rich Invest in That the Poor and the Middle Class Do Not
by Robert T. Kiyosaki, Sharon L. Lechter

Rich Dad, Poor Dad: What the Rich Teach Their Kids About Money - That the Poor and Middle Class Do Not!
by Robert T. Kiyosaki, Sharon L. Lechter

Positive Personality Profiles: Discover Personality Insights to Understand Yourself and Others
by Robert A. Rohm

What to Say When You Talk to Yourself
by Shad Helmstetter

The 7 Habits of Highly Effective Families
by Stephen R. Covey

Feel the Fear and Do It Anyway
by Susan Jeffers

Success Through a Positive Mental Attitude
by W. Stone

See You at the Top
by Zig Ziglar

Notes

Other Works By Samuel Blankson

How to Destroy Your Debts

Printed: 165 pages, 6.0 x 9.0 in, Perfect-bound
Download: PDF (1739 kb)
ISBN: 1-4116-2374-6
Copyright Year: © 2005 by Samuel Blankson
Language: English
Publisher: Lulu.com

If you are like me, you hate being in debt! Every month you watch, your money run out before the end of the month. You scrape around for fuel and grocery money, and then finally you hit the credit cards, hoping they hold sufficient funds. If you want to get out of this cycle of worry over debt, this book may be your answer. I say, "May," because although this book will definitely give you techniques for controlling, managing, and even getting out of debt altogether, it will not do the work for you. That will be up to you. This book will reveal how to destroy your debts, including your mortgage. It will also make clear to you how you can increase your income, and have confidence in your financial future. Your journey to financial freedom begins here.

The Practical Guide to Total Financial Freedom: Volume 1

Printed: 124 pages, 8.5 x 11.0 in, Perfect-bound
Download: PDF (7761 kb)
ISBN: 1-4116-2058-5
Copyright Year: © 2005 by Samuel Blankson
Language: English
Publisher: Lulu.com

The first part of a five volume series on creating Total Financial Freedom. In this volume, you will learn the foundations of wealth building, and how to secure your family and your wealth against disasters and losses. This series offers practical, effective, and easy to follow advice for securely and quickly building wealth. If you are thinking of buying this book, you probably want to be free. Free from the rat race, free from the boss, free from the wage trap, and free from the mediocrity and hopelessness of poverty and lack of options. Until now, you may have had no other way of achieving this within the next half a decade. This book will change all that forever. This book, unlike many self-help books out there, will actually tell you what to do in order to achieve Total Financial Freedom. You will find out exactly how I went about achieving Total Financial Freedom. If you read, learn, and apply the lessons in this book, you too will achieve Total Financial Freedom.

OTHER WORKS BY SAMUEL BLANKSON

The Practical Guide to Total Financial Freedom: Volume 2

Printed: 173 pages, 8.5 x 11.0 in, Perfect-bound
Download: PDF (31040 kb)
ISBN: 1-4116-2057-7
Copyright Year: © 2005 by Samuel Blankson
Language: English
Publisher: Lulu.com

The second part of a five volume series on creating Total Financial Freedom. In this volume, you will learn how to invest in Bonds, Stocks and Shares, and Funds. This series offers practical, effective, and easy to follow advice for securely and quickly building wealth. If you are thinking of buying this book, you probably want to be free. Free from the rat race, free from the boss, free from the wage trap, and free from the mediocrity and hopelessness of poverty and lack of options. Until now, you may have had no other way of achieving this within the next half a decade. This book will change all that forever. This book, unlike many self-help books out there, will actually tell you what to do in order to achieve Total Financial Freedom. You will find out exactly how I went about achieving Total Financial Freedom. If you read, learn, and apply the lessons in this book, you too will achieve Total Financial Freedom.

The Practical Guide to Total Financial Freedom: Volume 3

Printed: 143 pages, 8.5 x 11.0 in, Perfect-bound
Download: PDF (1716 kb)
ISBN: 1-4116-2056-9
Copyright Year: © 2005 by Samuel Blankson
Language: English
Publisher: Lulu.com

The third part of a five volume series on creating Total Financial Freedom. In this volume, you will learn how to invest in En Primeur Wine, Real Estate, Businesses, Life Insurances, Art, and Offshore investment opportunities. This series offers practical, effective, and easy to follow advice for securely and quickly building wealth. If you are thinking of buying this book, you probably want to be free. Free from the rat race, free from the boss, free from the wage trap, and free from the mediocrity and hopelessness of poverty and lack of options. Until now, you may have had no other way of achieving this within the next half a decade. This book will change all that forever. This book, unlike many self-help books out there, will actually tell you what to do in order to achieve Total Financial Freedom. You will find out exactly how I went about achieving Total Financial Freedom. If you read, learn, and apply the lessons in this book, you too will achieve Total Financial Freedom.

OTHER WORKS BY SAMUEL BLANKSON

The Practical Guide to Total Financial Freedom: Volume 4

Printed: 134 pages, 8.5 x 11.0 in, Perfect-bound
Download: PDF (3961 kb)
ISBN: 1-4116-2055-0
Copyright Year: © 2005 by Samuel Blankson
Language: English
Publisher: Lulu.com

The fourth part of a five volume series on creating Total Financial Freedom. In this volume, you will learn how to trade and invest in Momentum products. These instruments are high-risk products that offer high returns, but also the possibilities of high losses. You will learn how to limit those losses by reducing the risk using effective and practical methods. Options, Futures, High Yield Investment Programs, and Gambling are some of the exciting topics covered in detail. This series offers practical, effective, and easy to follow advice for securely and quickly building wealth. This book, unlike many self-help books out there, will actually tell you what to do in order to achieve Total Financial Freedom. You will find out exactly how I went about achieving Total Financial Freedom. If you read, learn, and apply the lessons in this book, you too will achieve Total Financial Freedom.

The Practical Guide to Total Financial Freedom: Volume 5

Printed: 322 pages, 8.5 x 11.0 in, Perfect-bound
Download: PDF (7143 kb)
ISBN: 1-4116-2054-2
Copyright Year: © 2005 by Samuel Blankson
Language: English
Publisher: Lulu.com

The last part of a five volume series on creating Total Financial Freedom. In this volume, you will learn how to lower your taxes, avoid paying unfair and unnecessary taxes, and how to move offshore and pay no taxes at all. This series offers practical, effective, and easy to follow advice for securely and quickly building wealth. If you are thinking of buying this book, you probably want to be free. Free from the rat race, free from the boss, free from the wage trap, and free from the mediocrity and hopelessness of poverty and lack of options. Until now, you may have had no other way of achieving this within the next half a decade. This book will change all that forever. This book, unlike many self-help books out there, will actually tell you what to do in order to achieve Total Financial Freedom. You will find out exactly how I went about achieving Total Financial Freedom. If you read, learn, and apply the lessons in this book, you too will achieve Total Financial Freedom.

OTHER WORKS BY SAMUEL BLANKSON

Living the Ultimate Truth, 2nd Edition

Printed: 166 pages, 6.0 x 9.0 in, Perfect-bound
Download: PDF (855 kb)
ISBN: 1-4116-2375-4
Copyright Year: © 2005 by Samuel Blankson
Language: English
Publisher: Lulu.com

Today most people live a poor example of a balanced life. The centuries of wisdom passed down from the great leaders of our past seem lost amid lives centred on minutia and selfishness. Today we care more about what we wear and where we are seen, than we do about discovering and Living the Ultimate Truth. Throughout the world, there is an imbalance in people's spirituality, consciousness, and inner harmony. This has taken a great toll on our environment, our health, and our happiness. Many are wondering around like lost sheep, seeking a shepherd in all the wrong places. Many false prophets have promised quick fixes to these problems, but if these solutions are not firmly rooted in The Creator, love, integrity and inner harmony, they are doomed to fail. This book is a reminder of all those virtues and universal principles that we need, to return to a balanced, harmonious, and happy life. You will learn to love yourself, love others, and finally find that inner peace you seek through spiritual growth.

Developing Personal Integrity, 2nd Edition

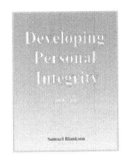

Printed: 118 pages, 6.0 x 9.0 in, Perfect-bound
Download: PDF (627 kb)
ISBN: 1-4116-2376-2
Copyright Year: © 2005 by Samuel Blankson
Language: English
Publisher: Lulu.com

In the field of human character development, integrity is the last frontier. Many people use the word, but few really know what real integrity is. This book breaks down the fundamental components of personal integrity and offers a path to attaining it. Like success or happiness, integrity is a journey not a destination. We can only measure how far on the path we are through the observation of our inner voice, the voice of our conscience, and through deep contemplation and reflection. This journey of personal excellence is not an easy one, and as a friend once said, "When peeling this onion, sometimes you cry." Nevertheless, in all great endeavours, the harder the struggle, the greater the victory will be.

OTHER WORKS BY SAMUEL BLANKSON

The Guide to Real Estate Investing

Printed: 117 pages, 6.0 x 9.0 in, Perfect-bound
Download: PDF (723 kb)
ISBN: 1-4116-2383-5
Copyright Year: © 2005 by Samuel Blankson
Language: English
Publisher: Lulu.com

If you have ever wanted to know how to make money from real estate, but could never find one source that listed and explained all the different options available to you, then your search is over. This book covers over 20 different ways of investing in real estate. You will find the author's style easy to understand and very practical. The section on self-build is so in-depth, that after reading it you will actually know how to build a house, and the section on REITs, Indexes, and REIT Options will leave your mind boggling at the potential profits available to you. This book also covers the conversional and popular methods of real estate investing as well. Therefore, whether you want to learn to develop real estate projects, build your own home, or simply rent a room in your house, this book will help you maximise your success and avoid the pitfalls.

Making Money with Funds

Printed: 79 pages, 6.0 x 9.0 in., Perfect-bound
Download: PDF (8769 kb)
ISBN: 1-4116-2671-0
Copyright Year: © 2005 by Samuel Blankson
Language: English
Publisher: Lulu.com

Today the world fund market is a multi trillion-dollar industry. There are many types of funds and as many reasons for choosing them. In this book, you will learn how Funds work, and how you, can make money with them.

How to make a fortune with Options trading

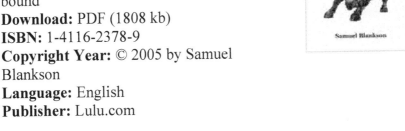

Printed: 59 pages, 8.5 x 11.0 in, Perfect-bound
Download: PDF (1808 kb)
ISBN: 1-4116-2378-9
Copyright Year: © 2005 by Samuel Blankson
Language: English
Publisher: Lulu.com

This is a practical book on winning in the Options trading market. Whether you are a sophisticated investor or a complete novice, this book is for you. The author takes complex ideas, and explains them in a way that is both practical and easily understood by anyone. Having used these techniques to achieve financial freedom, Mr Blankson now shares with you how he did it. There is no waffling here, just plain speaking and powerful techniques that anyone can apply.

OTHER WORKS BY SAMUEL BLANKSON

How to make a fortune on the Stock Markets

Printed: 190 pages, 8.5 x 11.0 in, Perfect-bound
Download: PDF (8769 kb)
ISBN: 1-4116-2379-7
Copyright Year: © 2005 by Samuel Blankson
Language: English
Publisher: Lulu.com

This book contains simple but effective techniques for achieving regular and consistent profits from stock trading. Unlike other books on the topic, it is not full of theory and projections, but practical advice learned the hard way, by trading personal hard-earned cash daily in the world's stock exchanges. Moreover, unlike other books on the subject, it is not about how to be a stock trader and trade other people's money, but on how to grow your own funds to a level where you will never have to work for anyone else again. This book contains real techniques used by the author to amass a fortune significant enough to have made him Financially Free. Now you too can use these simple but highly effective techniques to achieve the same results. Therefore, whether you are a professional trader or a total beginner, this book will show you how to achieve Financial Freedom through trading Stocks and Shares.

Tax Avoidance A practical guide for UK residents

Printed: 104 pages, 6.0 x 9.0 in, Perfect-bound
Download: PDF (355 kb)
ISBN: 1-4116-2380-0
Copyright Year: © 2005 by Samuel Blankson
Language: English
Publisher: Lulu.com

UK residents pay some of the highest taxes in the world. Most of these taxes are hidden through VAT and service charges. This guide clearly explains what taxes you are paying, and which ones you can and should avoid paying through claiming your allowed deductions and allowances. Prudent tax efficient estate planning is explained in detail, and hundreds of tax saving ideas are shared within these pages. Whether you are a qualified accountant or a non-professional, you will find this little guide an invaluable source of tax saving ideas and strategies.

Taking Action

Printed: 105 pages, 6.0 x 9.0 in, Perfect-bound
Download: PDF (1,095 kb)
ISBN: 1-4116-2735-0
Copyright Year: © 2005
Language: English
Publisher: Lulu.com

This is a book about taking action. This book will show you how to change your understanding of taking action to mean something you are doing NOW! When you change this focus in your life, you will release great powers. This book will show you how to tap into this phenomenal power and change your life.

OTHER WORKS BY SAMUEL BLANKSON

The Ultimate Guide to Offshore Tax Havens

Printed: 418 pages, 8.5 x 11.0 in, Perfect-bound
Download: PDF (12602 kb)
ISBN: 1-4116-2384-3
Copyright Year: © 2005 by Samuel Blankson
Language: English
Publisher: Lulu.com

This book is a detailed listing of all the known and not so commonly known Tax Havens, their benefits, and their suitability for relocation by the low tax seeker. If you are looking for ways to cut your taxes, there is no better way than to relocate to a low or no tax haven. The South East Asian Tsunamis and earthquakes have shown us that it is prudent to select the haven you will reside in carefully. Low taxes cannot be your only gauge for this task. This book will help you make that decision.

A must read for all who aspire to changing their lifestyles by relocating offshore. The havens are listed in geographical order, starting with the USA and ending with the South Pacific Islands.

Attitude

Printed: 418 pages, 6.0 x 9.0 in, Perfect-bound
Download: PDF (13700 kb)
ISBN: 1-4116-2382-7
Copyright Year: © 2005 by Samuel Blankson
Language: English
Publisher: Lulu.com

Attitude, so often misunderstood, yet so vital for success in every aspect of our lives. A positive attitude will guarantee happiness in your life, promotion and growth in your career or job, peace and joy in your family life, and in addition, a positive attitude has been scientifically proven to help extend your life expectancy. In this book, this essential success attribute is explained in detail. You will learn how to safeguard against positive attitude erosion, and learn how to build a positive mental attitude to help you achieve measurable success in every aspect of your life.

Uju

Download: MPG (6523 kb)
UPC: 4-3157-3526-2
Copyright Year: © 2004 by Samuel and Uju Blankson
Language: English
Publisher: Lulu.com

A six track EP with soulful R&B tracks with a pop flavour. This EP is bound to have you humming along addictively. For more info about the artist Uju, visit *www.uju-music.com* and look out for her forthcoming album.

OTHER WORKS BY SAMUEL BLANKSON

How to win at Greyhound betting

Printed: 68 pages, 8.5 x 11.0 in, Perfect-bound
Download: PDF (639 kb)
ISBN: 1-4116-2377-0
Copyright Year: © 2005 by Samuel Blankson
Language: English
Publisher: Lulu.com

Today, sports betting is a big industry for the bookmakers and organisers. Of all the people who benefit from sports racing, the "punters" (or in this case, you), are the last on the list of people who consistently gain. In fact, the greyhounds probably gain more from these races than most punters. Why is that? Well, there are many reasons, but most of them centre on these two things: lack of a proven system, and greed. This book closely examines these two points, and offers techniques and systems for achieving consistent wins in greyhound betting.

How to Win at Online Roulette

Printed: 81 pages, 6.0 x 9.0 in, Perfect-bound
ISBN: 1-4116-2570-6
Copyright Year: © 2005 by Samuel Blankson
Language: English
Publisher: Lulu.com

This is a guide to consistently winning at online Roulette. It is a simple and to the point writing about an amazing system for gaining an advantage at online Casinos. This book will show you how to make £1000 per day or more from online Roulette.

The Ultimate Greyhound Betting System

Download: MS Excel (233 kb)
Copyright Year: © 2005 by Samuel Blankson
Language: English
Publisher: Lulu.com

If you think there is no trustworthy betting system out there, then prepare to be proven wrong. This is the betting system described in the series *The Practical Guide to Total Financial Freedom,* and the book *How to win at Greyhound betting.* This semi-automatic system allows its user to achieve a minimum of 30% profits per week by following a proven statistical and rule based system betting on UK Greyhound races. The system only requires you to supply the race results and place the bets with your bookmaker. Armed with this incredible system, you will be able to beat the odds, and win one over the bookmakers.

Sixty Original Song Lyrics

Printed: 200 pages, 6.0 x 9.0 in, Perfect-bound
Download: PDF (1072 kb)
ISBN: 1-4116-2059-3
Copyright Year: © 2004 by Samuel Blankson
Language: English
Publisher: Lulu.com

This is a compilation of original song lyrics by Samuel Blankson. This book contains 60 of the songs he wrote in between 2000 – 2002. Having had some of these lyrics made into songs for an album (see *www.practicalbooks.org*), and several of them now on compilations, Samuel now shares these 60 song lyrics with you.

OTHER WORKS BY SAMUEL BLANKSON

Images of Kilimanjaro

Printed: 26 pages, 11 x 8.5 in, Coil-bound
Start Date: January 1st, 2006
Duration: 12 months
Copyright Year: © 2004 by Samuel Blankson
Language: English
Publisher: Lulu.com

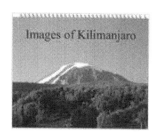

Kilimanjaro, the tallest freestanding mountain in the world, is captured here for you to feast your eyes on each month through 2006. Kilimanjaro is a source of life for Tanzania and Kenya locals, who live on its life giving rains and water. I had the honour of climbing this majestic mountain, and captured the essence of its allure and mystery through these pictures.

Images of Kilimanjaro

Printed: 53 pages, 8.5 x 11.0 in, Perfect-bound
Download: PDF (2573 kb)
ISBN: 1-4116-2016-X
Copyright Year: © 2004
Language: English
Publisher: Lulu.com

This is a book of pictures taken from Kilimanjaro. This is an accompanying book to the Calendar of the same name.

DEVELOPING PERSONAL INTEGRITY

The Bass by Samuel Blankson

Download: MPG (4811 kb)
Copyright Year: © 2004 by Samuel and Uju Blankson
Language: English
Publisher: Lulu.com

A sexy, R&B track with wicked beats and a deep baseline. With a melody and chorus that will stay with you for a long time, this addictive and catchy tune deserves your download (see *www.practicalbooks.org*).

Investing in En Primeur Wine

Printed: 88 pages, 6.0 x 9.0 in, Perfect-bound
Download: PDF (1,095 kb)
ISBN: 1-4116-2867-5
Copyright Year: © 2005
Language: English
Publisher: Lulu.com

Wine investing is not new, it has been going on for centuries. In more recent years (the last two centuries), government tax laws on alcoholic drinks have made buying wine a little more prohibitive to the investor who wants to keep them at home in his/her private cellar. Nevertheless, as usual, the market has found a way around this problem.

You can avoid taxes and V.A.T. (Value Added Tax) by buying fine wine on Bond (also called wine Futures or En Primeur). This book covers a simple and effective way in which anybody coming into the fine wine investing market place can safely securely and successfully select, and invest in En Primeur Wine.

OTHER WORKS BY SAMUEL BLANKSON

Eight Steps to Success

Printed: 105 pages, 6.0 x 9.0 in, Perfect-bound
Download: PDF (1,095 kb)
ISBN: 1-4116-2738-5
Copyright Year: © 2005
Language: English
Publisher: Lulu.com

We would all like to live a successful life, a life where our relationships and finances are a source of happiness and joy. This life is attainable by following timeless success principles. These principles have been forgotten by our fast food, fast-paced, reality TV society.

This book defines, explains, and shows you how to apply these principles and skills in your life to attain happiness, contentment, peace, joy, and prosperity. The eight fundamental virtues and skills required to succeed long-term in any endeavour, are explained in detail and in a style that everyone can understand and immediately apply.

The Eight Steps to Success is an inspirational book that will help you understand, acquire, hone, and apply the principles of success.

About The Author

An entrepreneur at heart, Samuel Blankson blends art, creativity, passion, business acumen, and financial expertise with careful planning and execution in the achievement of measurable results. He is an avid reader, writer, researcher, and securities trader.

He is an advocate of self-empowerment and an individual's ability to control their destiny through the achievement of personal freedom from economic, financial, spiritual, social, mental, and interrelationship restrictions. Samuel is constantly working to push the boundaries of personal achievements to their limits, recognising that these limits are only self-imposed.

Samuel has authored over twenty books (*How to Destroy Your Debts*, *Living the Ultimate Truth*, *Developing Personal Integrity*, *The Practical Guide to Total Financial Freedom volumes 1, 2, 3, 4 and 5*, and *Attitude* are some of these works). He has written over 100 songs, sixty of which are featured in *Sixty Original Song Lyrics*. He writes poetry, creates artwork, and works daily to express his creativity in many ways.

Having successfully run several businesses, Samuel diversified into securities trading over a decade ago, with great success. After learning from the masters of the time, Samuel progressed to develop his own methods and systems for successful trading. Today, he trades many financial instruments and has developed ways of successfully generating profits from his many investments.

A firm believer in knowledge sharing, Samuel travels the globe, teaching and sharing his personal knowledge with groups of friends, associates, and anyone who seeks to improve their life. This is the spirit of Samuel Blankson, a God centred philanthropist, overcomer, and high achiever.